Violin

SCHIRMER'S LIBRARY OF MUSICAL CLASSICS

Vol. 2080

VIOLIN CLASSICS

12 Pieces by 11 Composers
Advanced Level

For Violin and Piano

T0033808

ISBN 978-1-4234-2852-7

G. SCHIRMER, *Inc.*

DISTRIBUTED BY
HAL•LEONARD®
CORPORATION
7777 W. BLUEMOUND RD. P.O. BOX 13819 MILWAUKEE, WI 53213

CONTENTS

Chaconne

from the Partita No. 2 in D minor, BWV 1004

Johann Sebastian Bach
(1685–1750)

Violin

Violin

Violin

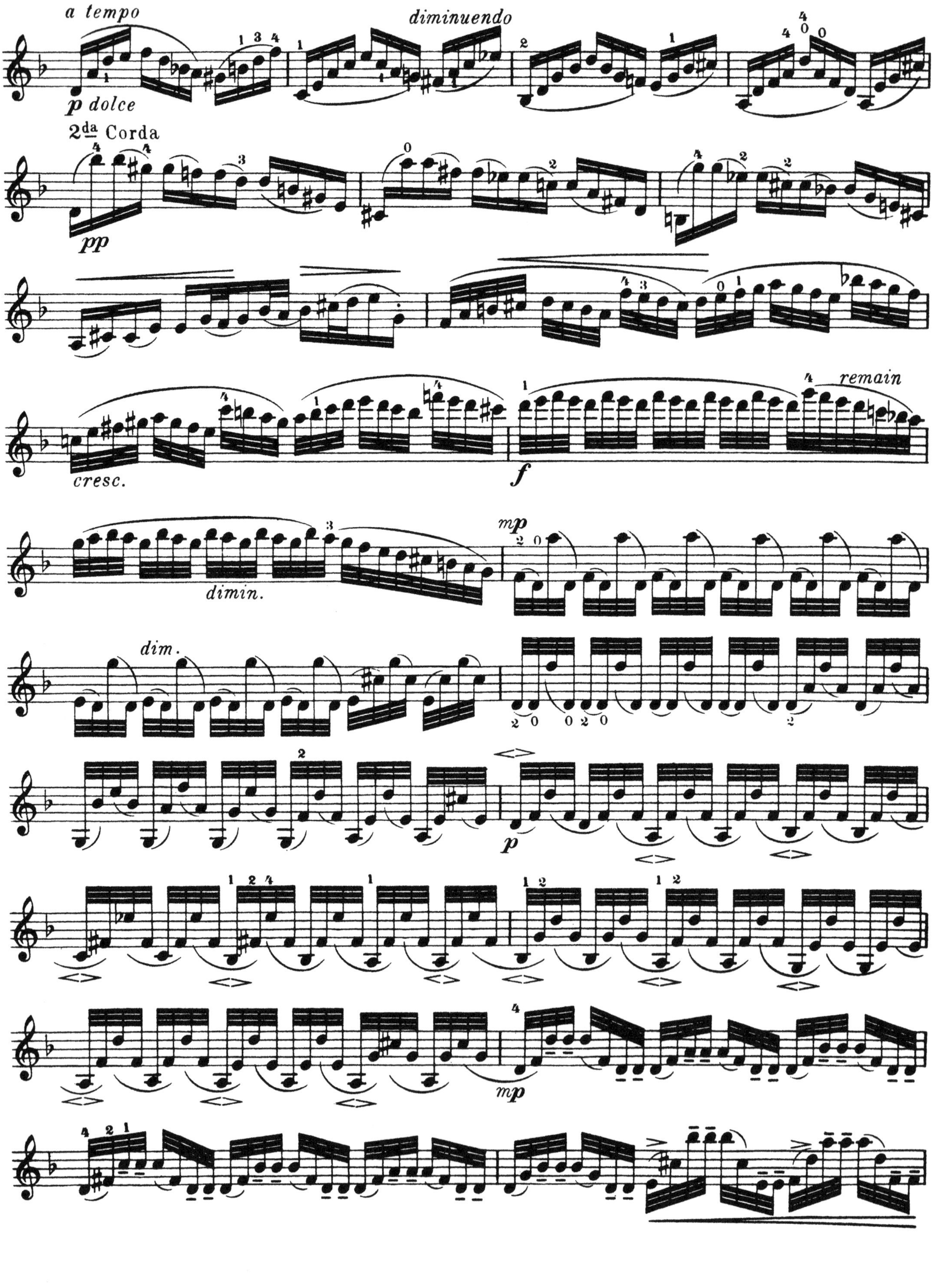
a tempo
p dolce
diminuendo
2da Corda
pp
cresc.
f
remain
dimin.
mp
dim.
p
mp

Violin

poco rit.
a tempo
cresc.
broad
dimin.
p sostenuto
cresc.

segue
dimin.
cresc.
rit. poco
cresc.
a tempo
mf sostenuto

Violin

pp
crescendo
p
cresc.
f
ff
mp
crescendo
cresc.
ff
rit.
pesante

Rondo

third movement from the Concerto No. 9 in A minor, Op. 104

Charles Auguste de Bériot
(1802–1870)

Violin

Allegretto moderato.

Violin

Violin

IV
dolce grazioso
III
cresc.
cresc.
cresc.
mf
p dolce
pp
cresc.
f
cresc.
poco a poco
f
dim.

nut
8
ff
Coda.
p molto leggiero
f
ff nut

(This page has been intentionally left blank to facilitate page turns.)

Scène de Ballet

Op. 100

Charles Auguste de Bériot
(1802–1870)

Violin
p molto espress.
cresc.
Tempo di bolero.
9
f
mf dolce
cresc.
f
leggiero
ff
sf
p grazioso

Violin

Violin

Violin

Valse moderato.
poco rall.
dim.
a tempo
cresc.
poco cresc.
cresc.
con eleganza

Violin

fz
cresc. poco a poco
fz
cresc.
f poco riten.
rit.
Adagio.
grandioso

Violin

stacc. ad lib.
con forza
Allegro appassionato.
Più animato.
cresc.

(This page has been intentionally left blank to facilitate page turns.)

Allegro moderato

first movement from the Concerto No. 1 in G minor, Op. 26

Edited and fingered by
Henry Schradieck.

Violin

Max Bruch
(1838–1920)

Violin

Solo.
mf espress.
cresc.
rit.
molto espress.
a tempo
sempre cresc.
ff
rit.
Un poco più lento.
molto espress.
ff
rfz
p
2da C
molto cresc.
sfz
ad lib.
p
Tempo I.
ff
ff
rfz
sfz
p
stringendo
poco

Violin
a poco
cresc.
cresc.
sempre cresc.
ff
Un poco più vivo.
Tutti.
ff
Viol.
sf
D
Bassi
ff
sf
sf
sf
sf
ff
marcato
sempre ff

Violin

LABORUM DULCE LENIMEN

G. SCHIRMER

Romance

Op. 11

Antonín Dvořák
(1841–1904)

Violin part edited by Rok Klopčič

Violin

*) ossia:

122
cresc.
(123)
rit.
f
125
a tempo
dim.
[p]
fz
dim.
pp
133
III
[p] molto espressivo
140
145
II
148
poco stringendo
cresc.
f
150
dim.
[p] in tempo
153
I
f
158
dim.
pp
162
dim.
pp
166
IV
pp

Violin

dim.
in tempo
ritard.
dim.
rit.
in tempo
dim.
poco stringendo e cresc.
dim e rit.
in tempo

Allegro non troppo

first movement from *Symphonie espagnole*, Op. 21

Edited by Leopold Lichtenberg

Édouard Lalo
(1823–1892)

*) Broad and sustained

Violin

Violin

ff
ff
f
f
mf
espress.
f
ff
ff
ff
nut
pesante
f
p
dolce espress.
cresc.
dolce
cresc.

*) Broad and sustained

Recitativo-Fantasia

third movement from the Sonate in A Major

César Franck
(1822–1890)

Violin

tr
ff poco animato
tr
tr
molto rit.
fff
a tempo moderato
pp
tranquillo
Piano
poco
dolciss. espress.
accelerando
a tempo
Piano
poco
accelerando
a tempo
mf drammatico
molto rall.
f
a tempo
dim.
p
Piano
poco accel.
dolciss.
cresc.
molto largamente e
f
cresc.
drammatico
fff
molto rit.
sempre fff
sempre rall.
dim.
Molto lento e mesto
non troppo dolce

Caprice in G minor

Op. 1, No. 16

Nicolò Paganini
(1782-1840)

Violin

Zigeunerweisen

Op. 20

Edited and fingered by
Philipp Mittell

Pablo de Sarasate
(1844–1908)

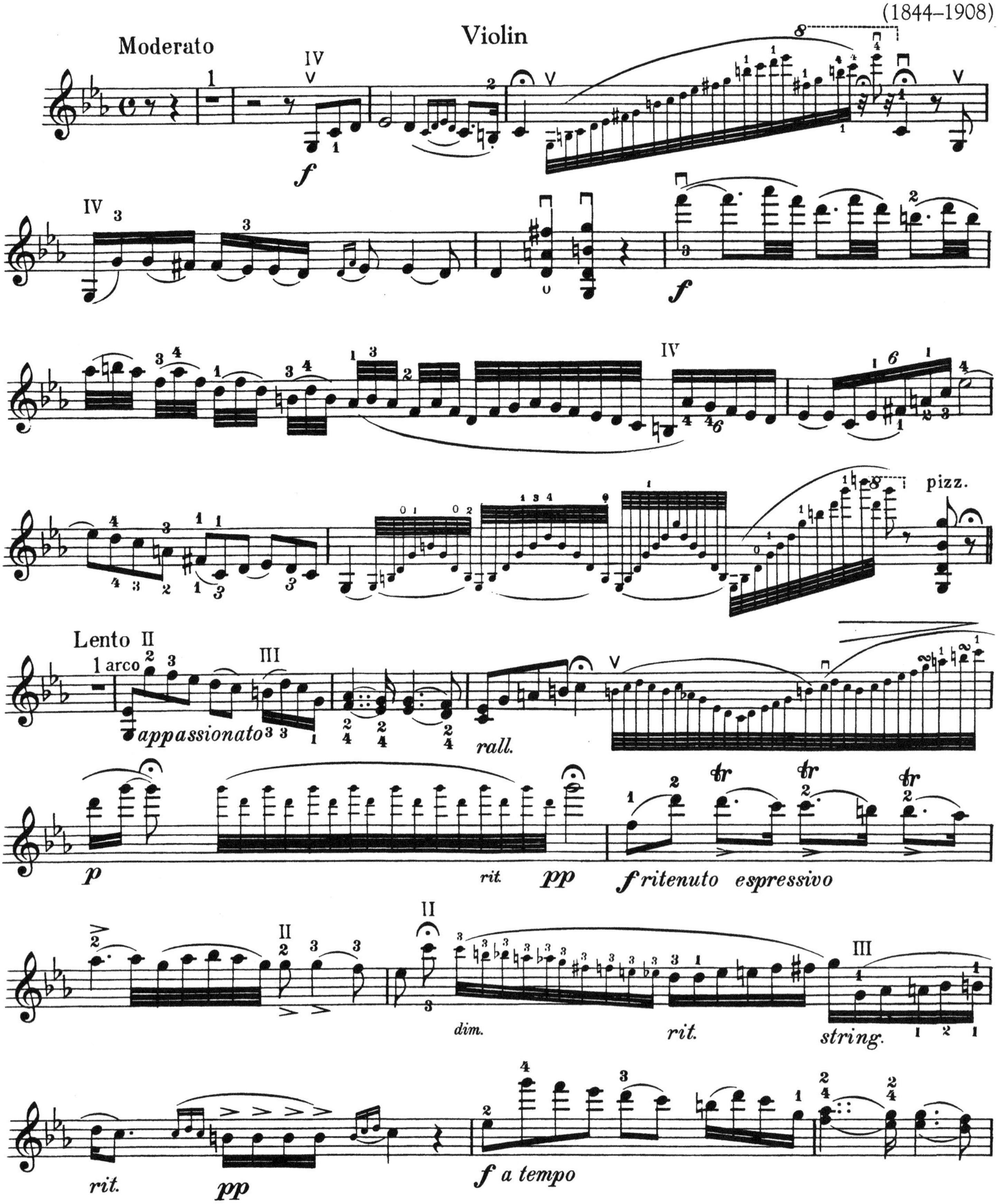

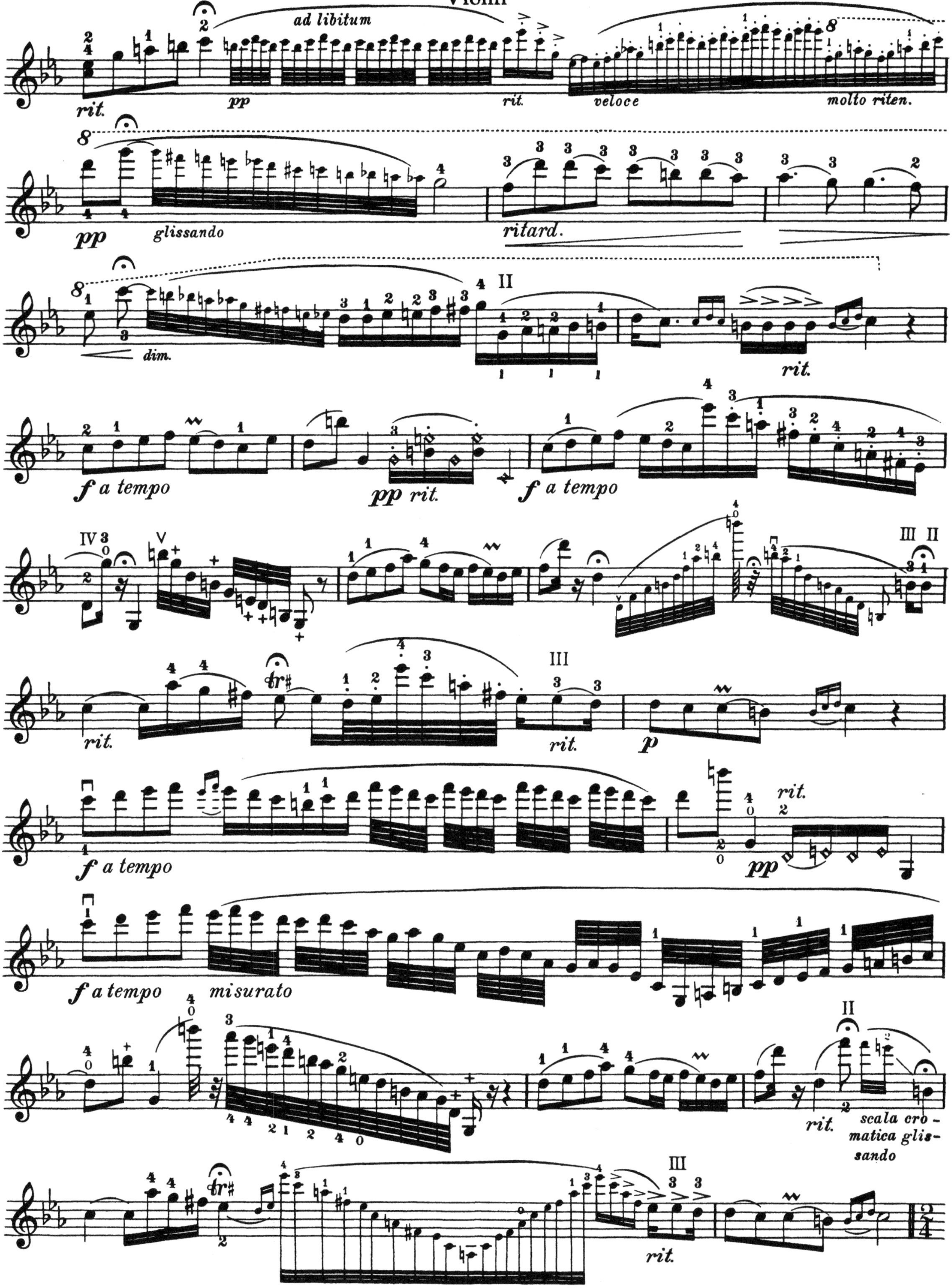
ad libitum
rit.
pp
rit.
veloce
molto riten.
pp
glissando
ritard.
dim.
rit.
f a tempo
pp rit.
f a tempo
rit.
rit.
p
f a tempo
rit.
pp
f a tempo
misurato
rit.
scala cromatica glissando
rit.

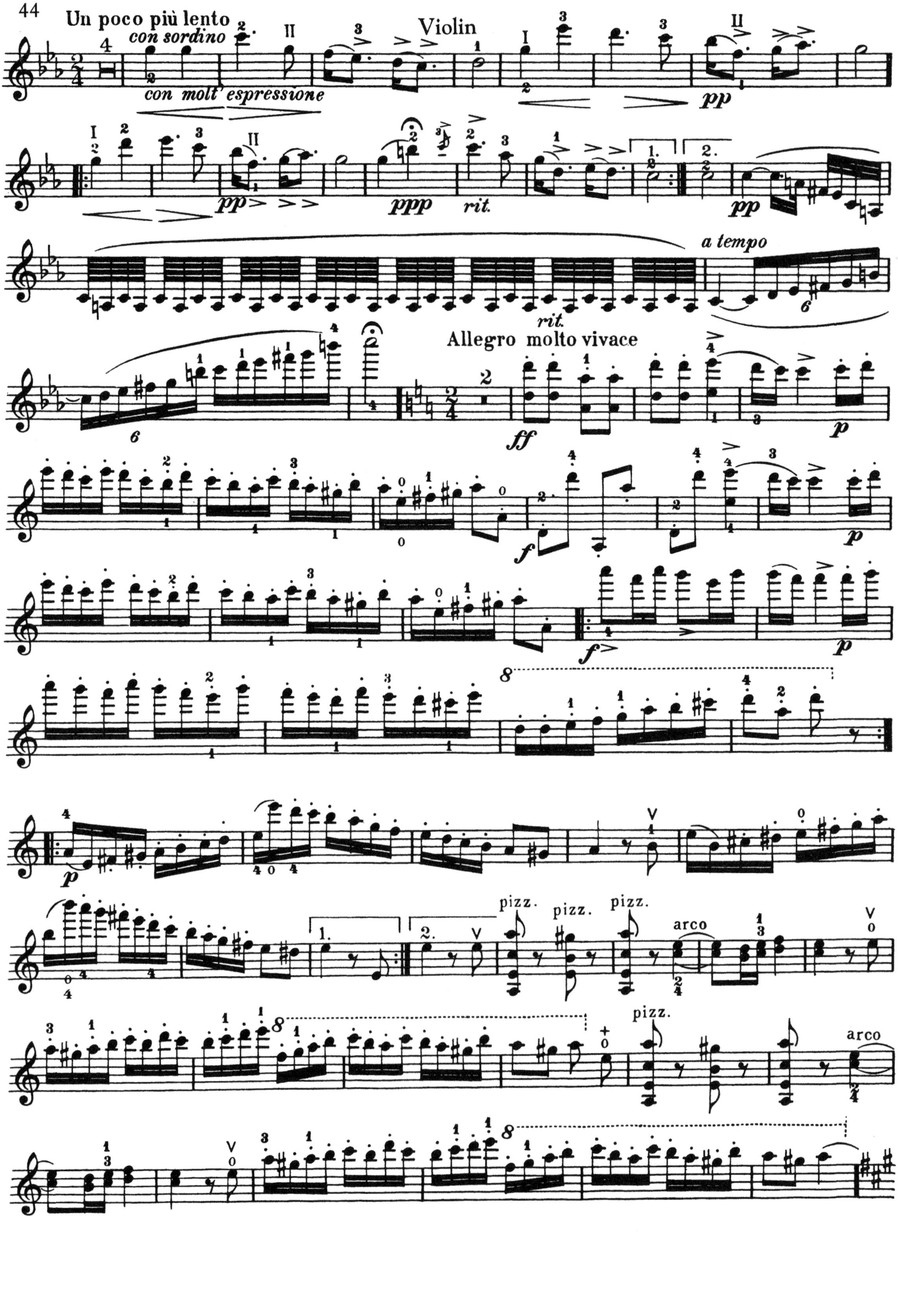
Un poco più lento
con sordino
con molt' espressione
pp
ppp
rit.
a tempo
rit.
Allegro molto vivace
ff
p
f
pizz.
arco

poco più pp
1.
2.
IV
f
pizz.
arco
animando
arco
animando sempre
cresc.
pizz.
ff

Agitato assai

third movement from the Concerto No. 22 in A minor, G. 97

Violin

Giovanni Battista Viotti
(1755–1824)

pt.
nut.
pt.
br.
cresc.
dim.
pt.
cresc.
IV

Violin

ff largamente
pt
p
f
fz
Tutti
ff

Violin

Violin

Concerto in E Major
RV 269 ("Spring")

Edited by Rok Klopčič

Violin

Antonio Vivaldi
(1678–1741)

Violin
THUNDER
45 The skies are dark; lightning flashes and thunder roars.
50
SO
CELLI
After the storm, the birds return with their song.
60
(mf)
tr
(f)
70
(mf)
80
p

Violin

THE SLEEPING GOATHERD

On the flowered meadow, the goatherd and his dog roam among the blossoming trees.

PASTORAL DANCE

Nymphs and shepherds dance to the bagpipes under the beautiful skies of spring.

160
(meno f)
170
simile
180
190
200
210

(This page has been intentionally left blank to facilitate page turns.)

Allegro molto appassionato

first movement from the Concerto in E minor, Op. 64

Allegro molto appassionato **Violin**

Felix Mendelssohn
(1809–1847)

Printed in the U.S.A. by G. Schirmer, Inc.

Violin

Solo.
II
cresc.
f
sf
sf restez.
sf
p
cresc.
sf
cresc.
f
p
cresc.
f
sf
sf
dimin.
sf
sempre di-
mi - nu - en - do
tranquillo.
pp
tranquillo.
pp
III.
p cresc. sf
sf
II.
cresc.

II.
a tempo.
II.
fp
rit.
cresc.
sf
cresc.
f
cresc.
leggiero.
p
cresc.
sf
p
pp
cresc.
sf
cresc. sf
IV
p leggiero
p
IV.
p
cre - - - scen - - do
ff
Tutti. Solo.
ff
con forza.
sf
IV. agitato.
p
cresc.
f Tutti.

Violin

Solo.
p tranquillo.
cresc.
Fl.
f
dim.
III.
II.
p dim.
sempre più p
al - - pp
sempre pp
cresc.
Cadenza ad libitum.
ff
f
Tempo I.

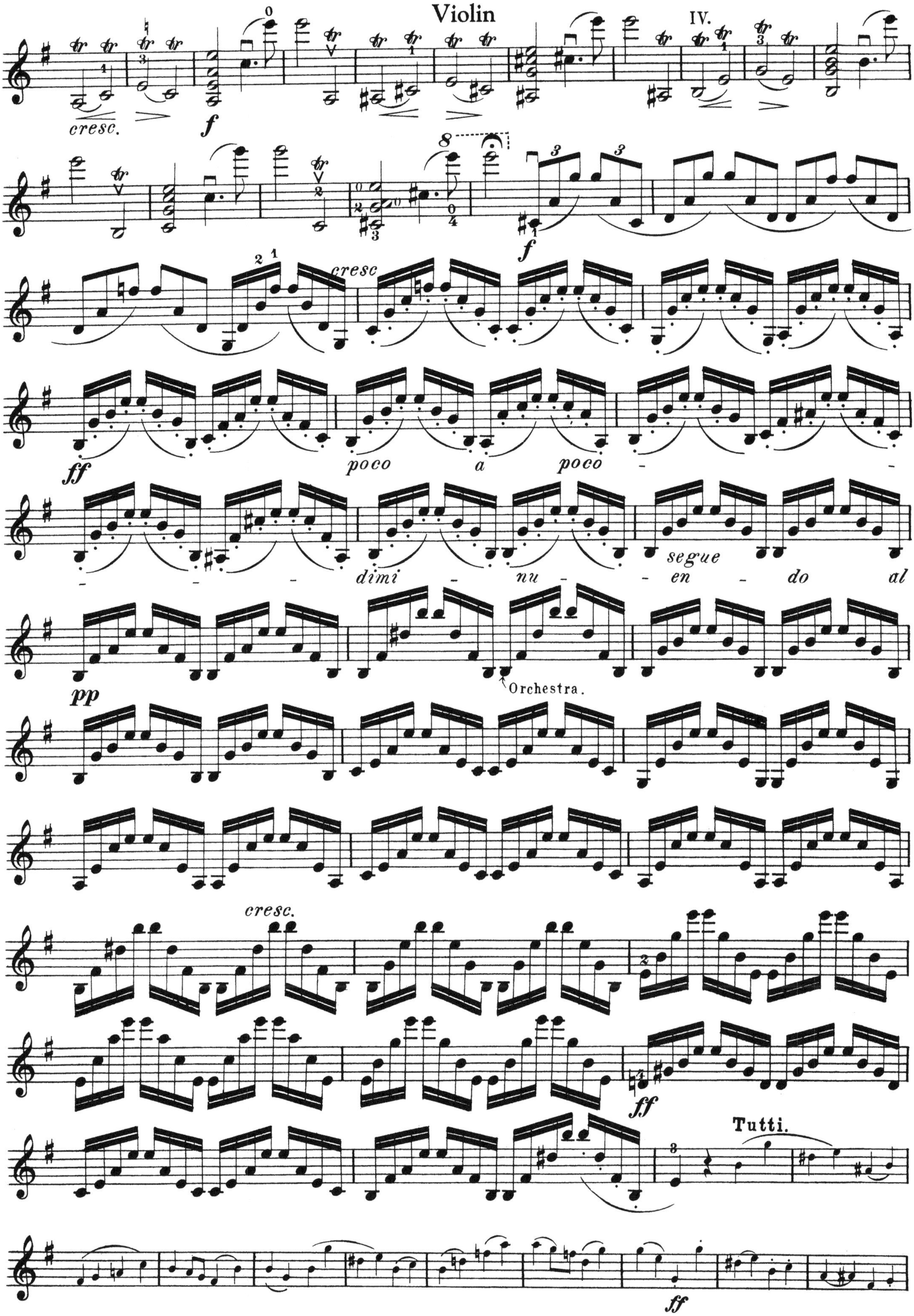
IV.
cresc.
f
cresc
ff
poco a poco
segue
dimi nu en do al
pp
Orchestra.
cresc.
ff
Tutti.
ff

Violin
II.
Solo.
mf
di - mi - nu - en - do sempre
più tranquillo.
pp
cresc.
III
II
dim.
pp
cresc.
cresc.
f
p
pp
cresc.
sf
sf
sf
più cresc.

Violin

IV.
cre
scen
do
II.
at the point.
Tutti.
Solo.
più Presto.
sempre più Presto.
cresc.
Presto.
cresc.
Tutti.
Fag.